Patty Lyons'

KNITTING
BAG OF
TRICKS

THE OFFICIAL
WORKBOOK

Hands-on exercises to improve your knitting skills

Includes stickers and illustrations by Franklin Habit

DAVID & CHARLES

www.davidandcharles.com

Color me in with cables, lace,
bright colors, stranded knitting. . .

Let your imagination fly!

Color in the needle to chart your progress through the lessons

8

7

This workbook belongs to

....

6

5

I've been knitting for .... years.

My biggest knitting challenge is

4

....

3

....

My knitting goals are

2

....

1

....

How it started...

KNITMOJI
STICKER
HERE

....

—

"KNITTING is the saving of life"

Virginia Woolf

Your Book About YOUR Knitting

When I was a kid, my favorite book was Dr. Seuss' *My Book about ME*. It was an interactive book that had questions with blanks to fill in, places to tape pictures, and boxes to color in. It was fun. But more than just being fun, it was my book to write all about my favorite topic (at least according to my mother) — ME!

This is YOUR book to write about your favorite topic — KNITTING!

When I am working with my students in a classroom, I'm employing all three prongs of learning: verbal, visual, tactile. In *Patty Lyons' Knitting Bag of Tricks*, I wanted to put a master knitting class in your hands. Thanks to my brilliant editor Carol Sulcoski, we have verbal covered (the words); thanks to my equally brilliant technical illustrator Linda Schmidt, we have the visual set (pictures); but tactile, the hands-on knitting, is the missing link. That's where this workbook comes in.

Think of this as a knitting party in your hands. Work it on your own or with a group of friends or at your local yarn shop. There will be mini patterns to work, charts, fill-in-the-blanks, pictures to color, and even stickers. And what workbook would be complete without the wit and whimsy of Franklin Habit illustrations?

I hope this is a workbook that can help you grow on your knitting journey. So, without further ado, it's your time to explore your knitting.

—

FIGHT FOR THE WHY AND BECOME A BETTER KNITTER!

How to Use Your Workbook

This workbook is meant to be worked hand in hand with *Patty Lyons' Knitting Bag of Tricks*. Keep the book handy and refer to it as you work through the lessons. If it's been a while since you read *Bag of Tricks*, you might want to review each chapter before diving into the correlating workbook lesson.

The workbook is divided into three sections:

❶ EXERCISES
❷ STICKERS
❸ MY WORK

Each lesson will correspond to a chapter of the book.

- You'll work a series of swatches that will allow you to practice every trick in the book.

- Since you'll be working on some swatches in more than one lesson, it's helpful to tag each swatch with its number. You can place swatches on a stitch holder or waste yarn so you don't run out of needles. Since some of the swatches will be seamed, it'll be helpful to use the same yarn for Swatches #6 through #13.

- Look for the "See also" tags that refer to a corresponding section of the book. This way you can remind yourself of instructions as you work.

- After each exercise, you'll find a "Swatchservations" section for notes and a question or two as a prompt. You can answer the questions or write about anything that is personal to your knitting. Don't rush this; it's helpful to refer to these notes as you grow.

Remember, this is all about learning and improving YOUR knitting. That means observations and notes. Examine your knitting. Think about both the process and the finished product. What would you like to improve? Is there a personal tip you need to remember?

And since as knitters we love visuals, there are also plenty of fun ways to decorate your journey. You'll have stickers and pictures to color and space for you to tape in yarn snips and add photos of your swatches. Grab those cute little picture printers, pull out your colored pens, and let your creativity flow.

EXERCISES

The journaling aspect of the workbook will be your most valuable tool. There's no such thing as thinking too much about your knitting!

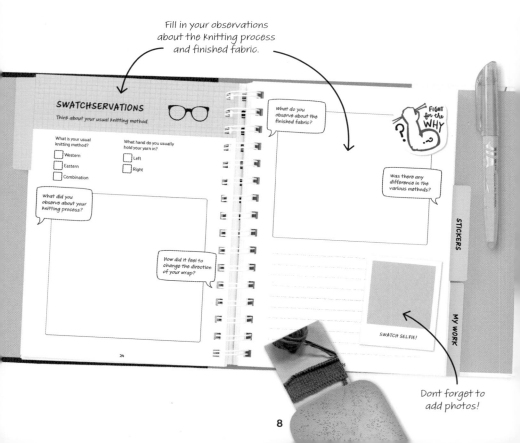

Fill in your observations about the knitting process and finished fabric.

SWATCHSERVATIONS
Think about your usual knitting method.

What is your usual knitting method?
- Western
- Eastern
- Combination

What hand do you usually hold your yarn in?
- Left
- Right

What did you observe about your knitting process?

How did it feel to change the direction of your wrap?

What do you observe about the finished fabric?

FIGHT for the WHY

Was there any difference in the various methods?

SWATCH SELFIE!

STICKERS

MY WORK

Don't forget to add photos!

24

STICKERS

What workbook would be complete without adorable stickers to decorate it? Use them anywhere your inspiration strikes. You'll see a few outlines suggesting sticker placement along the way.

MY WORK

The final section of the workbook is all about you: your knitting, your projects (current and future), and everything you'd like to learn. Use this section to launch your year of skill building.

You'll have plenty of pages to track upcoming projects and knitting goals. Don't forget to start by listing the tricks you'll use in each pattern.

Let's cast on!

Track your 12 months of skill building projects.

SWATCH LIST

Each lesson will direct you on what swatches to work and how:

SWATCH #1

Cast on 25 stitches in a non-superwash wool (use in Lessons 1 and 6).

SWATCH #2

Cast on the number of stitches on your yarn ball band plus eight (use in Lesson 2).

SWATCHES #3, #4, and #5

Try three new fibers (use in Lesson 3).

NOTE: Use the same type of yarn for **Swatches #6** through **#13**.

SWATCH #6

Cast on 25 stitches (use in Lessons 4, 5, and 7).

SWATCH #7

Cast on 28 stitches (use in Lessons 4, 6, and 7).

SWATCH #8

Cast on 15 stitches (use in Lessons 4 and 7).

SWATCH #9

Cast on 21 stitches (use in Lessons 4 and 6).

SWATCH #10

Cast on 37 stitches in color A, using the circular needle of your choice (use in Lesson 6).

SWATCH #11

Cast on 42 stitches (use in Lesson 7).

SWATCHES #12 and #13

Cast on 20 stitches (use in Lesson 7).

—

MAKE YOUR
STITCHES
BE YOUR

(RHYMES WITH STITCHES)

Before We Begin:
Learn Where We Are

This lesson is the foundation for our entire workbook. Through these exercises you will explore two vitally important things: how you currently knit, and the DNA of knitting itself — the knit and the purl.

Let me ask you this: are you a continental knitter (who holds the yarn in their left hand) or a thrower (who holds the yarn in their right hand)? Did you have to pick up your knitting to check? That's because muscle memory is so strong that many of us knit without thinking, so much so that we aren't even sure which hand we hold our yarn in.

This is your chance to focus on how you knit. Watch the direction you wrap your yarn and the path the yarn travels; notice where your leading leg is. Pay attention to how you hold your needles and how you tension your yarn.

Okay, I feel like I can hear you right through the pages. You want to skip these exercises, don't you? You want to jump ahead to the "hard part" or the "fun part." After all, you're thinking, I know how to knit and purl.

Trust me: don't skip this section. In fact, if you work only one lesson from the whole workbook, work this one. (Have I ever lied to you?) You're going to learn some vital things about your knitting, and we're going to build on this knowledge as we work together through the exercises.

You know the song: Let's start at the very beginning. It truly is a very good place to start.

EXERCISE: KNITS AND PURLS

It's time to rock our knits and purls.

Remember your knitting structure. It's simply a loop **pulled** through another loop versus a loop **pushed** through another loop. Let's see how that works by knitting a series of stitch patterns in your regular knitting style.

SWATCH #1

Cast on 25 stitches in a non-superwash wool.

SECTION 1 (First garter stitch section)

Knit 8 rows.

SECTION 2 (Second garter stitch section)

Purl 8 rows.

SECTION 3 (Stockinette stitch section)

Row 1 (RS): Knit.

Row 2 (WS): Purl.

Rep these 2 rows three more times (a total of 8 rows).

SECTION 4 (Ribbing section)

Row 1 (RS): *K1, p1; rep from * to last st, k1.

Row 2 (WS): P1, *k1, p1; rep from * to end of row.

Rep these 2 rows two more times (a total of 6 rows).

Row 7 (RS): *K1, p1; rep from * to last st, k1.

NOTE: you are knitting the knits and purling the purls.

SECTION 5 (Seed stitch section)

NOTE: this section starts on a WS row.

Next row: *K1, p1; rep from * to last st; k1.

Repeat last row seven more times, ending with a RS row.

NOTE: you are knitting the purls and purling the knits.

Do NOT bind off when you have finished the last row. Leave the live stitches on the needle.

See also: **BAG OF TRICKS** STITCH ANATOMY

SWATCHSERVATIONS

Now that you've completed knitting these sections, it's time to examine your knitting to see what it can tell you. Lay out your swatch on a flat surface with good lighting and take a look.

1. Knit garter
2. Purl garter
3. Stockinette
4. Ribbing
5. Seed stitch

On the following pages, write a bit about your knitting process as well as the finished product.

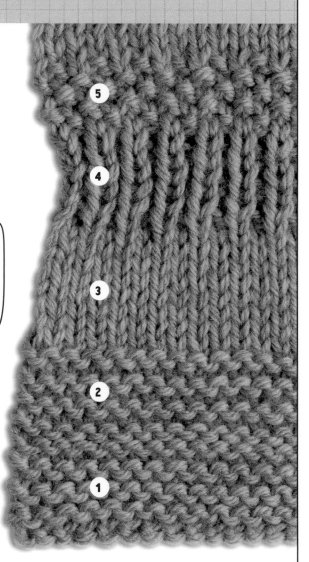

15

GARTER STITCH

What did you notice as you worked?

Did working the knit garter feel different from working the purl garter?

What do you observe about the finished fabric?

Any width difference between the knit garter section and the purl garter section?

Yes ☐ No ☐ If yes, add measurements: _____

Any difference in stitch quality?

Yes ☐ No ☐

Any height differences?

Yes ☐ No ☐ If yes, add measurements: _____

What goals do you have for improving your garter?

....
....
....
....
....
....

Do you feel like you are a loose, tight, or average knitter?

What was your knitting style working this section?

Flip the swatch over and look at the reverse stockinette. Do you see any gaps between rows?

Yes   No

What do you observe about the finished fabric?

Are there any uneven stitches?

Yes   No

Looking at the right (public) side of the section, how does the right edge look?

What goals do you have for improving your stockinette?

PURL   KNIT

RIBBING

Next we'll examine the ribbing section.

What did you observe about your knitting process?

Does it feel comfortable and efficient to switch between knits and purls?

What else can you observe about your knitting?

Is there a difference in space between the purl and the knit vs the knit and the purl?

Yes ☐   No ☐

How much does the fabric pull in from the stockinette?

What goals do you have for improving your ribbing?

....

....

....

....

....

Now let's look at the last section,
the seed stitch.

> What do you observe
> about the finished fabric?

Does it feel the same as
working 1x1 ribbing?

Yes ☐ No ☐

If not, how is it different?

Does the fabric pull in
the same as ribbing?

Yes ☐ No ☐

Write the seed stitch width and ribbing width measurements here:

Seed stitch width ☐   Ribbing width ☐

What goals do you have for improving your seed stitch?

....

....

....

....

....

How it's going

KNITMOJI
STICKER
HERE

PICTURES & THOUGHTS

Anything you learned about your knitting?

Is your knitting loose or tight?

DON'T FORGET
YOUR STICKERS!

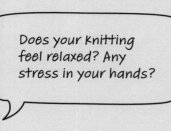

Does your knitting feel relaxed? Any stress in your hands?

SWATCH SELFIE!

EXERCISE: STITCH MOUNT

(It's all about how the yarn travels!)

The best thing you can do to understand your knitting is to experiment. In this exercise we will be digging into the most important knitting truth of all:

- Where you put the needle affects your now (do I twist a stitch or leave it open?); and
- The direction you wrap the yarn affects your future (how the stitch sits on the needle for the next row).

Let's put this truth to the test by experimenting with three different styles of knitting: Western, Eastern, and combination. When beginning this section of the swatch, we are assuming that the existing stitches are already sitting with the leading leg in front.

SWATCH #1 *[CONTINUED]*

WESTERN (your leading leg is in front)

(WS): Purl through the front loop, wrapping yarn OVER to under.

(RS): Knit through the front loop, wrapping yarn UNDER to over.

TRANSITION

(WS): Purl through the front loop, wrapping your yarn UNDER to over (this is the Eastern/combination purl).

EASTERN (your leading leg is now in the back)

(RS): Knit through the back loop, wrapping OVER to under.

(WS): Purl through the back loop, wrapping UNDER to over.

COMBINATION

(RS): Knit through the back loop, wrapping UNDER to over.

(WS): Purl through the front loop, wrapping UNDER to over.

See also: **BAG OF TRICKS** HOW OUR STITCHES ARE BUILT

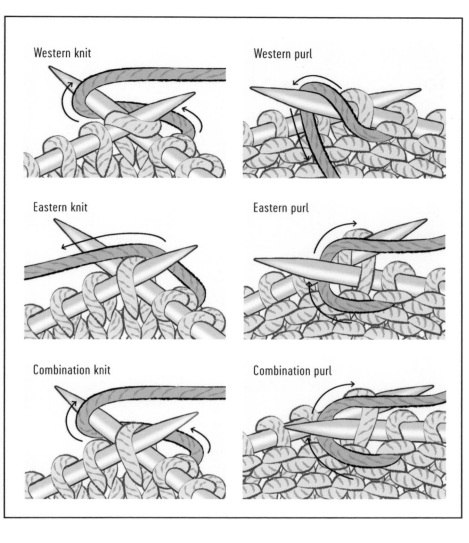

Western knit

Western purl

Eastern knit

Eastern purl

Combination knit

Combination purl

what did the horse
say to the stitches?

SWATCHSERVATIONS

Think about your usual knitting method.

What is your usual
knitting method?

☐ Western

☐ Eastern

☐ Combination

What hand do you usually
hold your yarn in?

☐ Left

☐ Right

What did you
observe about your
knitting process?

How did it feel to
change the direction
of your wrap?

What do you observe about the finished fabric?

Was there any difference in the various methods?

SWATCH SELFIE!

EXERCISE: STITCH MOUNT

To twist or not to twist!

Time to kick it up a notch and test your skills. When you realize you can wrap your yarn any which way and **still** work across a row without twisting a stitch, you feel your confidence grow. When you can do that with your eyes closed, you feel like a superhero.

When you advance the stitch you're about to work to the tip of the left needle, you should be able to feel the "face" of the stitch. That's how you know if the leading leg is in front or back. (Remember the little stitches straddling the horse?)

Let's see how you do.

SWATCH #1 *(CONTINUED)*

After completing the combination section, your leading leg is now in back.

(RS): Knit, putting the needle in the hole and wrapping the yarn any way you want. Make it hard on yourself by wrapping the yarn on some stitches moving under to over and on other stitches moving over to under.

Now your stitches will have some leading legs in front and others in back. Can you work across the row without twisting a stitch?

(WS): Purl, putting the needle in the hole and wrapping the yarn any way you want. Make it hard on yourself by wrapping the yarn on some stitches moving under to over, and some over to under.

Now your stitches will have some leading legs in front and others in back. Can you work across the row, putting the needle in the hole, without looking?

(RS): Work across this row feeling for the stitch face. Can you put the needle in the hole and not twist a stitch? Wrap in your usual direction.

(WS): Purl across in your own style.

Do not bind off. We will return to this swatch in Lesson 6.

See also: **BAG OF TRICKS** HOW OUR STITCHES ARE BUILT

SWATCHSERVATIONS

Think about how it felt when you worked
rows with different stitch mounts.

STITCH MOUNTS

Did you work across the row without twisting a stitch?   Yes ☐   No ☐

How did it feel to wrap differently for the knit?
How did if feel for the purl?

EYES SHUT

Did you feel the face of the stitch?   Yes ☐   No ☐

Did you work across the row without twisting a stitch?   Yes ☐   No ☐

27

—

IF YOU **DON'T** *HAVE TIME* TO SWATCH

SAVE TIME TO RIP OUT YOUR SWEATER!

The Truth Is Out There!

My mother told me that part of growing up is loving and accepting who you are. That's how I feel about gauge swatches.

When we are itching to cast on for a new project, our self-deception knows no bounds. You know what I'm talking about: "But I'm a good knitter," "I'm using the same yarn the pattern calls for," and my personal favorite, "I'll just cast on a few stitches, and if I'm in the ballpark — it's GO time!"

You can't accept who you are until you know who you are. In Lesson One, you focused on getting to know your own knitting. Now it's time to practice your technique. After reviewing your spacing and your measuring cup, you'll compare your technique both flat and in the round.

Remember our goals from the gauge chapter. First create a fabric that you love, make sure your swatch is an accurate predictor of your fabric (read: non-liar), and lastly, measure accurately and make all your "cookie math adjustments."

Speaking of cookies, let's start by making sure we are using our measuring cup correctly.

EXERCISE: MEASURING CUP

Before thinking about gauge or measurements, you'll work in stockinette, paying attention to your measuring cup and space between friends.

SWATCH #2 (USE IN LESSON 2)

Using a circular needle in the size recommended by the ball band, cast on 12 more stitches than the gauge on the ball band. For example, if the ball band states 18 stitches per 4in/10cm, you'll cast on 30 stitches: 18 plus 12.

Work in stockinette stitch for a few inches or centimeters.

- Check your measuring cup.
- Remember to advance to the tip of the left needle and size to the shaft of the right needle.

See also: **BAG OF TRICKS** YOUR MEASURING CUP

SWATCHSERVATIONS

Feel your stitches on the needle. Do they feel tight?

Yes ☐   No ☐

Pull down on the fabric. Do you see space underneath?

Yes ☐   No ☐

If you don't feel like you are on the right "measuring cup" for the stitch size you made, try the knitting exercise in Bag of Tricks/End of the Perfect Tool: Your Measuring Cup.

EXERCISE: THE SPACE BETWEEN

Once you've mastered sizing your stitches, pay attention to the space between the stitches. Don't forget to keep those needles connected, like an X, and slide off your stitch in the direction your left needle is pointing.

SWATCH #2 *(CONTINUED)*

Keep working in stockinette for a few more rows.

See also: **BAG OF TRICKS** — THE SPACE BETWEEN STITCHES

SWATCHSERVATIONS

What did you observe about your knitting process?

Does the next stitch advance easily?   *Yes* ☐   *No* ☐

How does it feel when you remove your new stitch?

What do you observe about the finished fabric? Turn your work around. Do you see any gaps between the rows?   *Yes* ☐   *No* ☐

Describe any changes in the quality of your stitches.

EXERCISE: FLAT VERSUS IN-THE-ROUND SWATCH

Now it's time to see how our purl stitch changes our stockinette gauge. For this gauge exercise we'll skip ahead and use a technique taught in Chapter Six.

SWATCH #2 *[CONTINUED]*

NEXT SECTION (flat)

Keep working flat in stockinette for a few more rows, ending on a RS row.

TRANSITION

(WS): Knit. This will create a purl ridge to divide your flat swatch from your speed swatch that will simulate working in the round.

SPEED SWATCH

Continue working the same swatch, but change to knitting a speed swatch to simulate knitting in the round for approx. 4in/10cm more.

ENDING SWATCH

Measure out a length of the working yarn a bit wider than your swatch. Break the yarn, put the tail on a tapestry needle, and thread the yarn through the live loops to remove the swatch from the needle. Tie a knot at the end of the yarn.

See also: **BAG OF TRICKS** SWATCHING THE LAZY WAY

...How it's going

KNITMOJI STICKER HERE

SWATCHSERVATIONS

You've taken the time to practice your knitting technique so you can create a fabric you like. You've also swatched honestly to get a sample that is an accurate predictor of your gauge. Your final step is to measure.

Using a ruler, measure your stitch and row gauge of your unblocked swatch for flat and in the round.

First measure your stitch and row gauge unblocked.

Fill in unblocked gauge:

Unblocked Gauge

Stitch gauge flat: ⬜ sts per 4in/10cm

Row gauge flat: ⬜ rows per 4in/10cm

Stitch gauge in the round: ⬜ sts per 4in/10cm

Row gauge in the round: ⬜ rnds per 4in/10cm

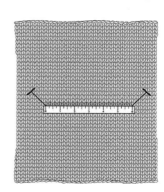

Block your swatch and after it's fully dry, measure again. If you're not sure which blocking technique to use, refer to the ball band. Most yarns do very well with a wet block.

Using a ruler, measure your stitch and row gauge of your blocked swatch for flat and in the round.

Fill in blocked gauge:

Blocked Gauge

Stitch gauge flat: ⬜ sts per 4in/10cm

Row gauge flat: ⬜ rows per 4in/10cm

Stitch gauge in the round: ⬜ sts per 4in/10cm

Row gauge in the round: ⬜ rnds per 4in/10cm

See also: **BAG OF TRICKS** HOW TO MEASURE YOUR SWATCH

PICTURES & THOUGHTS

Did you learn anything about your knitting?

SWATCH SELFIE!

Were you using your measuring cup?

How was your exit path? Did your friends stay together?

Notes

Did you learn anything about your gauge?

Was your "in the round" swatch different from the flat one?

Did your fiber change when blocked and if so, how?

Remember, swatching is knitting (the thing we love!) — plus it tells us everything we need to know about our ingredients. Look at measuring as the very last step, not the main goal.

Now that we have a fabric we love, a non-liar swatch, and our gauge, it's time for the cookie math. Pour yourself a glass of milk, grab a bag of chocolate chip cookies and a calculator, and let's dive in with a review of Patty's Magic Triangle of Gauge.

EXERCISE: THE MAGIC TRIANGLE OF GAUGE

Fill in number (e.g. 200) and descriptions (e.g. sts) in the formulas below.

THE THREE MAGIC FACTORS
[ANSWERS ON PAGE 128]

1. If you know the number of **stitches** and you know the width of the garment in **inches/centimeters**, you can figure out your **gauge**.

Suppose you lost the first page of your pattern that listed gauge, but you know you should have 200 stitches around the chest, and the chest is 40in/101.5cm. How do you figure out your gauge?

PATTY'S MAGIC TRIANGLE OF GAUGE

Stitches or Rows
"So, Really"

Inches (cm)   Gauge
"I'll (continue to)" X "Guess"

Formula: ☐ (what: ☐) ÷ ☐ (what: ☐) = ☐ (gauge)

2. If you know your **gauge** and you know the width of the piece that you want in **inches/centimeters**, you can figure out how many **stitches** to cast on.

Say you want a scarf that will be 8in/20cm wide. Your gauge is 5 stitches per 1in/2.5cm. How do you calculate how many stitches you need?

Formula: ☐ (what: ☐) × ☐ (what: ☐) = ☐ (stitches)

3. If you know your **gauge** and you know how many **stitches** you have, you can figure out how wide your piece will be **inches/centimeters**.

This is where the real fun begins! Say you didn't match the pattern gauge and you wanted to know what size you'd get if you followed the pattern using your gauge, 5.25 stitches per 1in/2.5cm. If the pattern calls for 200 stitches around the chest, how do you know what the chest measurement will be?

Formula: ☐ (what: ☐) ÷ ☐ (what: ☐) = ☐ (in/cm)

See also: **BAG OF TRICKS** DIFFERENT GAUGE, SAME COOKIE MATH

Time to see just how much you can do with your simple cookie formulas. Let's play with size. Crack out that magic triangle and enjoy the power!

SIZE ADJUSTMENTS WITH GAUGE (ANSWERS ON PAGE 128)

1. Overall size change

You have swatched until you get a fabric you LOVE, but your gauge doesn't match the pattern. You actually want an in-between size. How do you pick the best pattern size to follow?

The sweater back and front for Size 2 is 18in/46cm wide (99 stitches at the chest), and for Size 3 is 20in/51cm (110 stitches at the chest). Pattern gauge is 22 stitches per 4in/10cm. You'd like the front and back pieces to be closer to 19in/48.5cm wide and your gauge is 21 stitches per 4in/10cm.

Since your gauge is LARGER than the patterns, to get an in-between size, which size should you try at your gauge — the second (99 stitches) or the third (110 stitches)?

☐ sts

What will be the width of the sweater back in inches/centimeters when you follow the above size in your gauge?

Formula: ☐ (what: ☐) ÷ ☐ (what: ☐) = ☐ (in/cm)

2. Change a portion of the sweater

The back and front of your size sweater are each 18in/46cm, but you'd like an extra 1in/2.5cm at the hip for both front and back (approx. 2in/5cm total around). You'd like to change the needle size to get a different gauge for your hips.

The sweater front has 99 stitches at the hip and the pattern gauge is 22 stitches per 4in/10cm.

What gauge should you aim for to create the width you'd like in the hip in the sweater front and back?

Formula: ☐ (what: ☐ ÷ ☐ (what: ☐) = ☐ (gauge)

(Rounded) How many stitches per 4in/10cm? ☐ (stitches)

EXERCISE: MORE STITCH GAUGE FUN

What else can cookie math do for us? This time I'm not going to tell you if the formula uses multiplication or division; it's all on you.

MISSING GAUGE INFORMATION (ANSWERS ON PAGE 128)

Your sweater pattern lists a stockinette gauge of 24 stitches per 4in/10cm. However, it uses an allover lace pattern without a bit of stockinette in it! Since you know it's far better to swatch in the sweater's stitch pattern, how do you find the lace gauge?

What you know: The schematic shows the size you want is 19in/48.5cm for front and back. There are 129 stitches for the chest.

What is your gauge in lace?

Fill in the blanks and circle x or ÷.

Formula: ☐ (what: ☐) x ÷ ☐ (what: ☐) = ☐ (gauge)

(Rounded) How many stitches per 4in/10cm = ☐

YOUR STITCH GAUGE CALCULATIONS

Take a pattern you're working on. Any changes you'd like to make in gauge or width? Try it here.

Notes

....

....

....

....

....

....

EXERCISE: ROW GAUGE FUN

Behold the awesome power of row gauge! Many knitters have trouble matching row gauge or want to change the length of a sleeve or alter waist shaping. Knowing that those changes are easily within your control makes you feel like a knitting superstar.

1. Same shape, different row gauge **(ANSWERS ON PAGE 129)**

The pattern row gauge is 28 rows per 4in/10cm. Your row gauge is 24 rows per 4in/10cm. You'd like to keep the same number of decreases to the waist over the same number of inches used in the pattern.

The pattern has six decrease rows. You work the first decrease row and then repeat that decrease row every eighth row five more times.

What you need to know: How many rows does the pattern use in the shaping zone? How many inches/centimeters are in the shaping zone? How many rows do you need to work in YOUR row gauge? How should you distribute the five shaping rows?

1) How many rows were used in the shaping zone after the first decrease?

5 times $\times$ ☐ (rows) = ☐ rows total

2) How many inches/centimeters are in the shaping zone using the pattern gauge?

☐ (rows) $\div$ ☐ (gauge) = ☐ in/cm

3) How many rows in YOUR gauge are in the shaping zone?

☐ (inches) $\times$ ☐ (gauge) = ☐ rows

4) Divide number of rows in your shaping zone by the number of shaping rows in your gauge.

Spread out the five remaining decreases to waist:

☐ (rows) $\div$ ☐ (shaping rows) = ☐ rows to repeat

Round down to nearest even number.

Repeat decrease row every ☐ rows 5 more times.

See also: **BAG OF TRICKS** SAME FINISHED SIZE, DIFFERENT GAUGE

2. Different length, different row gauge **(ANSWERS ON PAGE 129)**

Your pattern has long sleeves, but you'd like to shorten them AND you have a different row gauge. Multiply the number of inches/centimeters you want in your shaping zone by your row gauge. Then do the same math to spread them out.

The pattern gauge is 28 rows per 4in/10cm. Your gauge is 24 rows per 4in/10cm. You'd like to keep the same number of increases for your sleeve, over a different number of inches/centimeters than the pattern uses.

After working your cuff, the pattern has you work a total of ten increase rows. You work the first increase row and then repeat that increase row every twelfth row nine more times, then work even until the sleeve measures 18½in/47cm. You'd like a sleeve that is only 16½in/42cm long. This means you'd like to eliminate 2in/5cm from your shaping zone.

What you need to know: How many rows does the pattern use in the shaping zone? How many inches/centimeters are in the shaping zone? How many rows do you need to work in YOUR row gauge over a different number of inches? How should you distribute the remaining nine shaping rows?

1) How many rows were used in the shaping zone after the first increase?

9 times $\times$ ⬚ (rows) = ⬚ rows total

2) How many inches/centimeters are in the shaping zone?

⬚ (rows) $\div$ ⬚ (gauge) = ⬚ (in/cm)

3) How many inches/centimeters are in YOUR shaping zone?

⬚ (pattern shaping zone) $-$ ⬚ (in/cm you're removing) = ⬚ (in/cm)

4) How many rows in YOUR gauge are in YOUR shaping zone?

⬚ (in/cm) $\times$ ⬚ (gauge) = ⬚ (rounded down to even number) ⬚

See also: **BAG OF TRICKS** DIFFERENT FINISHED SIZE, DIFFERENT GAUGE

5) Divide number of rows in shaping zone by number of shaping rows.

Spread out nine remaining increases for sleeve:

[ ] (rows) ÷ 9 (shaping rows) = [ ] rows to repeat

Round down to the nearest even number.

Repeat decrease row every [ ] rows nine more times

How many inches/centimeters are used in your final shaping zone?

9 (remaining shaping rows) × [ ] (repeat) = [ ] total rows used

[ ] total rows used ÷ [ ] (your row gauge) = [ ] (in/cm)

YOUR ROW GAUGE CALCULATIONS

Take a pattern you're working on. Any changes you'd like to make in gauge or length? Try it here.

Notes

....

....

....

....

....

....

....

...How it's going

KNITMOJI
STICKER
HERE

—

KNITTING PATTERNS,
LIKE LIFE, ARE BEST
WHEN WE DON'T TRY TO
OVERCOMPLICATE THEM.

What Are We Making and What Are We Making It With?

My husband loves to cook. He also loves reading recipes and playing with ingredients. For the life of me, I can't understand the joy of sitting down to read a recipe or tasting ingredients with no finished meal in mind. On an entirely different subject — I love to knit. I also love reading patterns and swatching different yarns with no specific project in mind. Ah well, to each his own, I say!

This lesson is about what we are making and what we are making it with. First up is our most beloved ingredient, yarn.

Time to understand the joy of playing with yarn and to learn how wonderful it is to swatch for the joy of swatching. With no project in mind, you are just seeing what that yarn does. This is all about understanding yarn properties. I promise that this will help you make more informed yarn choices for your next project.

Go to your stash or borrow some yarn from a friend, but challenge yourself to try a fiber you've never used. Let's see what happens.

SWATCHES #3, #4 AND #5

Pick out three different fibers of a similar gauge.

- Animal fiber or animal fiber blend (wool, alpaca, etc.)
- Synthetic fiber or synthetic fiber blend (acrylic, nylon, rayon from bamboo, etc.)
- Plant fiber or plant fiber blend (cotton, hemp, linen, etc.)

Swatch the same stitch pattern in each. Start with a couple of inches or centimeters of stockinette and then go into a stitch pattern. It can be cables, lace, basketweave, moss stitch, any stitch pattern you like.

SWATCHSERVATIONS

What do you think of the feel of each finished fabric? Shake it, stretch it, hold it against your skin. Does it hold its shape? Is it soft, scratchy, stiff, floppy?

How did the same stitch pattern behave in different fibers? What are the pros and cons of each?

Animal Fiber:

Add sample
yarn snips

Synthetic Fiber:

Plant Fiber:

Is it a grower?

Block your swatch and let it dry. Measure the full width and length of your swatch.

Animal fiber swatch: ☐ (width) ☐ (length)

Synthetic fiber swatch: ☐ (width) ☐ (length)

Plant fiber swatch: ☐ (width) ☐ (length)

Now it's time to see what your stitch pattern and fiber will do with gravity. Remember, a little swatch will not weigh the same as a full garment, scarf, or shawl.

Hang each swatch (a pants hanger works great). Add some weights to the bottom of your swatch. I use earrings that hurt my ears, but you can also use binder clips.

Let the swatch hang overnight. Remove the weights, let it rest flat for an hour or so, measure it again.

SWATCHSERVATIONS

Animal fiber swatch: ☐ (width) ☐ (length)

Synthetic fiber swatch: ☐ (width) ☐ (length)

Plant fiber swatch: ☐ (width) ☐ (length)

Were there any changes in the width and length of your swatch?

The relationship between weight and yardage matters. It will greatly affect how your garment hangs. Imagine you knit a scarf that seemed the perfect length and then after wearing if for a few hours you look like Dr Who. Or the sweater that fit you like a dream for the first 30 minutes has now grown down to your knees.

If you have a ball band for your yarn, look at the weight and yardage. Compare them all.

Apples to Apples

NOTE: You might have to multiply to make sure you are comparing apples to apples. For example, if you are comparing three yarns, make sure you are comparing the same total weight:

Yarn 1 = 100g = 247yds/226m

Yarn 2 = 100g = 139 yds/127m

Yarn 3 = 50g = 97yds/89m

You would convert Yarn 3 to a 100g skein by doubling the measurements so your comparison is accurate.

Yarn 1 = 100g = 247yds/226m

Yarn 2 = 100g = 139 yds/127m

Yarn 3 = 100g = 194yds/178m

Length and Weight of Yarns:

Animal fiber swatch: ☐ g = ☐ yds/ ☐ m

Synthetic fiber swatch: ☐ g = ☐ yds/ ☐ m

Plant fiber swatch: ☐ g = ☐ yds/ ☐ m

Weight of each swatch:

Animal fiber swatch: ☐ g

Synthetic fiber swatch: ☐ g

Plant fiber swatch: ☐ g

If this swatch was for a sweater, and you needed 30 times the amount of yarn used for each swatch for your sweater, how would the weight of each fiber compare?

Animal fiber swatch: ☐ (swatch weight) x 30 = ☐ (sweater weight)

Synthetic fiber swatch: ☐ (swatch weight) x 30 = ☐ (sweater weight)

Plant fiber swatch: ☐ (swatch weight) x 30 = ☐ (sweater weight)

PICTURES & THOUGHTS

What was the biggest surprise in comparing fibers?

What kinds of projects would work best with each type of fiber?

What did you learn about each different fiber you swatched?

Notes

....

....

....

....

....

....

PLANT

ANIMAL

SYNTHETIC

DON'T FORGET
YOUR STICKERS!

EXERCISE: CHEST MEASUREMENTS

Measure once, rip NEVER — picking the right size

Even if you have never knit a sweater before, you might someday!
When you do, you want to pick the right size. A set-in sleeve can be the
trickiest sweater fit to get right, so let's use that for our example:

Instead of trying to take all your body measurements, let's focus on two:

FULL CHEST: ☐ in/cm

UPPER TORSO: ☐ in/cm

Now you've got to add your desired ease to your upper torso. We're going to use two to four inches (or five to ten centimeters), a pretty typical amount of ease, for our example. The actual measurement plus ease will be your sweater size.

See also: **BAG OF TRICKS** TIP 1 AND 2

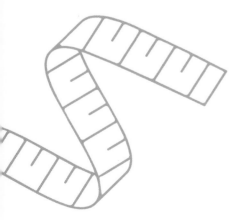

Let's use the sweater schematic as an example. Say your full chest measures 43in/109cm and your upper torso is 40in/101.5cm. Adding a few inches of ease to your upper torso gives us a range of 42in/106.5cm to 44in/112cm. Looking at the finished measurements at the bottom, we see that the sixth size, 43½in/110.5cm, would be a great pick.

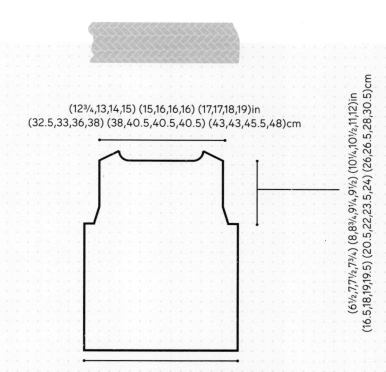

(12¾,13,14,15) (15,16,16,16) (17,17,18,19)in
(32.5,33,36,38) (38,40.5,40.5,40.5) (43,43,45.5,48)cm

(6½,7,7½,7¾) (8,8¾,9¼,9½) (10¼,10½,11,12)in
(16.5,18,19.5) (20.5,22,23.5,24) (26,26.5,28,30.5)cm

(16,17½,18¼,19) (20¼,21¾,23¼,24) (26¼,27,29,31¼)in
(40.5,44.5,46.5,48.5) (51.5,55,59,61) (66.5,68.5,73.5,79.5)cm

Finished Measurements

Chest: (32,35,36½,38) (40½,43½,46½,48) (52½,54,58,62½)in
(81.5,89,92.5,96.5) (103,110.5,118,122) (133.5,137,147.5,159)cm

NOTE: If you had added ease to your full chest measurement instead of the upper torso (giving you a range of 45in/114.5cm to 47in/119.5cm), you might have been tempted to choose the seventh size, 46½in/118cm. However, that size most likely would be too wide in the shoulders.

EXERCISE: MEASURING A SWEATER THAT FITS YOU

Remember, a sweater schematic shows the size of the finished garment. If you have trouble picking the best size to make from your body measurements, it's helpful to compare finished garment measurements.

Find a sweater or top (or several) that fits you well and record the garment measurements on the facing page.

See also: **BAG OF TRICKS** TIP 3 AND 4

Now compare the measurements of the sweater that fits with the measurements in the pattern. Try checking the armhole depth and cross back measurement of the sweater size you picked (based on your upper torso measurement plus ease) against the measurements of the sweater that fits you well. Your upper torso measurement is a skeletal measurement which connects to other skeletal measurements like armhole depth and cross back.

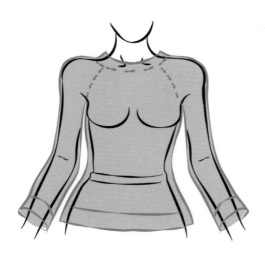

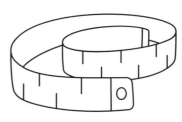

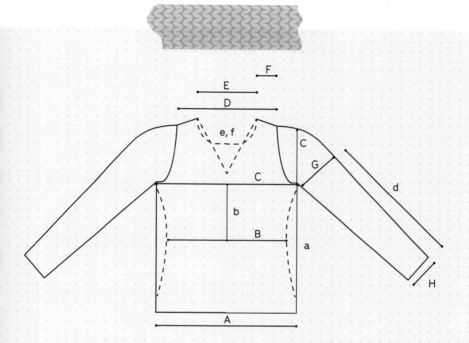

Finished Sweater Width

A = Hip _____

B = Waist _____

C = Chest _____

D = Crossback _____

E = Neck _____

F = Shoulder _____

G = Upper arm _____

H = Cuff _____

Finished Sweater Length

a = Body length to armhole _____

b = Armhole to waist _____

c = Armhole depth _____

d = Arm length _____

e = Crew neck depth _____

f = V-neck depth _____

...How it's going

KNITMOJI STICKER HERE

Better to have

KNIT & RIPPED

THAN NEVER TO
HAVE KNIT
AT ALL

Let's Get This Party Started!

Rarely have I found an element of knitting that is more complained about but less worked on than our cast-on. A bad cast-on can ruin our work. It can be too tight or too sloppy. It can have a rounded start or an icky (that's the highly technical term) end, yet most knitters don't seem interested in practicing the cast-on.

We love to knit and we will work endlessly to refine our lace, cables, our colorwork, but sail right past the cast-on to get to the "fun" part. In this lesson we are going to slow down and enjoy finding the perfect start.

These exercises are all about practicing the long tail and cable cast-on fixes from your bag of tricks. These cast-ons represent the two main families, single strand and double strand. I hope these exercises will light a fire under you to discover the world of cast-ons waiting for you.

Grab your yarn and needles and let's make some perfect starts.

And just to make your little product-driven hearts happy, these perfected cast-ons will grow into your practice swatches for later lessons.

EXERCISE: IMPROVE YOUR LONG TAIL CAST-ON

Before you get fancy with your long tail cast-on, let's take this time to improve the basics. This swatch will grow into your increase and decrease lesson and then will help you perfect your bind-off.

You'll need a worsted weight or heavier yarn in a light color, a needle in a size appropriate to your yarn weight, and some thin crochet cotton or sock yarn.

CAST-ON-FOLLIES

SWATCH #6 (USE IN LESSONS 4, 5, AND 7)

Cast on 25 stitches, practicing our four fixes and our one sanity saver.

Sanity Saver: Use some thin scrap yarn to help you keep track of your cast-on stitches. Try moving the scrap yarn every five stitches.

FOUR FIXES

☐ Measure out your yarn

☐ Skip the slip knot

☐ Put that tail in a butterfly to rid the unraveling

☐ Use your finger to space those stitches

See also: **BAG OF TRICKS** LONG TAIL CAST-ON

EXERCISE: FIX A DROPPED LONG TAIL CAST-ON STITCH

Now that we have created a perfectly measured and spaced long tail cast-on, it's time to practice wrecking it! You will create a lovely small garter edge for your swatch by knitting the first WS row. But you didn't think we'd skip dropping a stitch, did you?

SWATCH #6 *(CONTINUED)*

Remember, it doesn't matter what stitch, knit or purl, you are working on the first row; the long tail cast-on itself presents as a purl row. So don't forget to turn the swatch around to pick up your dropped cast-on stitch as a knit stitch.

Instructions: Knit 10 stitches, drop a cast-on stitch, turn the swatch around, and fix the dropped stitch. Now turn the swatch back around and knit to the end of the row.

Leave the live stitches on the needle or a stitch holder. You will continue working this swatch in Lesson 5.

EXERCISE: LONG TAIL CAST-ON IN PATTERN

Time to kick it up a notch and apply all you've learned to a perfect cast-on in pattern — one that uses both knits and purls. This swatch will grow into your technique swatch for Lesson 6.

You'll need a worsted weight or heavier yarn and needle in a size appropriate to your yarn.

SWATCH #7 (USE IN LESSONS 4, 6, AND 7)

Cast on 28 stitches in pattern.

Cast-on: (K3, p2) x 5, k3.

Row 1 (WS): *P3, k2; rep from * to last 3 sts, p3.

Leave the live stitches on the needle or a stitch holder. You will continue working this swatch in Lesson 6.

See also: **BAG OF TRICKS** LONG TAIL CAST-ON NEXT LEVEL

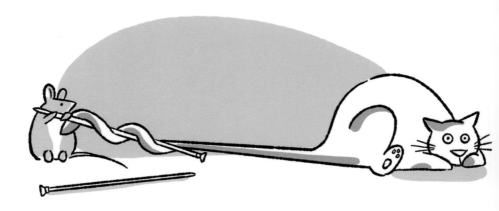

SWATCHSERVATIONS

What do you think of your newly improved long tail cast-on? Do you have a favorite fix?

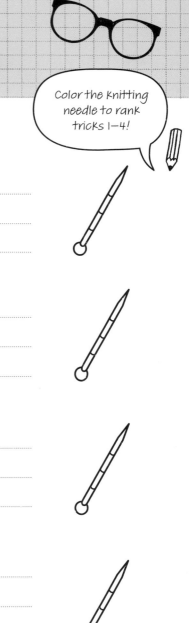

Color the knitting needle to rank tricks 1–4!

Measure Yarn and Space Stitches

....

....

....

Rid the Unraveling

....

....

....

Pick Up Dropped Long Tail Cast-On Stitch

....

....

....

Cast On in Pattern

....

....

....

PICTURES & THOUGHTS

what did you learn about your cast-on?

what projects would you use a long tail cast-on for?

When might you want to cast on in pattern?

...How it's going

KNITMOJI STICKER HERE

Long tail cast-on

Cast-on in pattern

SWATCH SELFIE!

SWATCH SELFIE!

Notes

....
....
....
....
....
....
....

EXERCISE: CABLE CAST-ON IN PURL

Now it's time to turn your attention to the second "desert island" cast-on, the delightful cable cast-on. Before we practice both the knit and purl, we'll make a lovely purl cast-on edge. This swatch will grow into your mini cardi swatch for Lesson 6.

> See
> also: **BAG OF TRICKS**   CABLE CAST-ON

SWATCH #8 (USE IN LESSONS 4 AND 7)

Cast on 15 stitches in purl cable cast-on. Practice your improved start and use the YO trick for your square end.

Begin with the improved start:

1) Using the long tail start, give your single twist and cast on one knit stitch, then turn work around to begin casting on the rest, using a cable cast-on in purl.

Cast on 12 more stitches – 14 sts.

Finish with your improved end:

2) Cast on the fifteenth stitch and use the yarnover (YO) trick to get a clean end.

Row 1 (RS): Knit.

Row 2 (WS): Purl.

Repeat these two rows two more times.

Leave the live stitches on the needle or a stitch holder. You will continue working this swatch in Lesson 7.

EXERCISE: CABLE CAST-ON IN PATTERN

You've practiced your purl cast-on stitches; now let's add in the knit for a stunning knit 1/purl 1 cast-on. The alternating cable cast-on leaves a rounded edge and makes a great alternative to tubular cast-on.

SWATCH #9 (USE IN LESSONS 4 AND 6)

Cast on 21 stitches in knit 1/purl 1 cable cast-on. Practice your improved start and YO trick for your square end, but this time in knit instead of purl.

Begin with the improved start:

1) Using the long tail start, give your single twist and cast on one stitch, then turn work around to begin casting on the rest using cable cast-on in pattern. You'll have one knit and one purl already on your needle, so start with a knit stitch.

Cast-on stitches: (K1, p1) x 9 – 20 sts cast on.

Finish with your improved end:

2) Cast on the twenty-first stitch and use the YO trick to get a clean end.

Row 1 (RS): *K1, p1; rep from * to last st, k1.

Row 2 (WS): *P1, k1; rep from * to last st, p1.

Repeat these two rows one more time.

Row 5 (RS): Knit.

Row 6 (WS): Purl.

Continue working in stockinette for 12 rows, ending with a WS row.

Leave the live stitches on the needle or a stitch holder. You will continue working this swatch in Lesson 6.

SWATCHSERVATIONS

What do you think of your newly improved cable cast-on?
Do you have a favorite fix?

Color the skein sections to rank tricks 1—4!

Fix the start with long tail cast-on

Fix the end of the cast-on in purl

Fix the end of the cast-on in knit

Cast on in pattern

PICTURES & THOUGHTS

what did you learn about your cast-on?

Cast-on purl

Cast-on pattern

SWATCH SELFIE!

SWATCH SELFIE!

EXERCISE: OTHER TWO-STRAND CAST-ONS

Hopefully, you're now starting to think about how many wonderful ways there are to start your project. You have perfected your long tail cast-on, but there are many others to explore.

For example, there is a large family of cast-ons that use two strands of yarn. One strand creates the edge and one creates the stitch on the needle. You can use two different colored strands, too, to get interesting effects.

Try experimenting with other cast-ons and make a list here. Take notes and jot down ideas for when you might want to use them.

Here are a few two-strand cast-ons to get you started: Italian, German Twisted, and Channel Island. What others can you find and try?

CAST-ON NAMES

EXERCISE: OTHER ONE-STRAND CAST-ONS

The cable cast-on belongs to the other main family of cast-ons: those that use one strand and two needles. Challenge yourself to play with these as well.

Try experimenting with other cast-ons and make a list here. Take notes and jot down ideas for when you might want to use them.

CAST-ON NAMES

Here are a few one-strand cast-ons to get you started: knitted cast-on, crochet cast-on, picot cast-on. What others can you find and try?

—

WHEN WE
MEMORIZE,
WE CAN
FORGET

WHEN WE
UNDERSTAND,
WE
NEVER FORGET

LESSON 5 — INCREASES AND DECREASES

Time to Break the Rules!

My favorite way to practice new techniques is to play with swatches. In this lesson you'll get to practice every increase and decrease taught in the book in one fun-filled, action-packed swatch. Take your time, knit, rip, try again. Experience the joy of knitting with no goal other than to enjoy learning about your knitting.

Grab your book and refer to it often. You will have both words and a chart, so try them both. As you work mindfully through your swatch, remember all we learned about increases and decreases.

In the first half of your swatch, consider the two universal rules of decreasing. Think about rule #1 as you REALLY pay attention to what stitch your needle enters first and what the result is. And of course, remember your old friend universal rule #2, the needle must go in the hole, as you appreciate when to break that rule and why. Last but not least, recall the universal rule of slipping. Think about what leaves a stitch open and what makes it twist.

In the second half of your swatch, it's time to rock your increases. You'll get a chance to practice your three families of increases: those worked between two stitches, into a stitch, and into the row below.

Grab your knitting and let's start breaking rules like an artist.

EXERCISE: DECREASES

CONTINUE WITH SWATCH #6

(continued from Lesson 4; use in Lessons 6 and 7)

Continue working with the long tail cast-on and Row 1 swatch from Lesson 4. You already cast on in Lesson 4, so you're ready to start working from your chart. In the first half of the swatch you'll get a chance to try out every decrease. Written instructions are below; if you prefer to work directly from a chart, I've included one as well.

Row 1 (RS): Knit.

Row 2: Purl to last 4 sts, Eastern p2, p2.

   Eastern Purl

Row 3: K2, SSK #1, k17, K2TOG, k2—23 sts.

   SSK Variation #1

Row 4: Purl.

Row 5: K2, SSK #2, k15, K2TOG, k2—21sts.

   SSK Variation #2

Row 6: Purl.

Row 7: K2, one move SSK, k13, K2TOG, k2—19 sts.

   One Move SSK

Row 8: Purl.

Row 9: K2, SK2P, k9, K3TOG, k2—15 sts.

   SK2P & K3tog

Row 10: Purl.

Row 11: K6, CDD, k6—13 sts.

   CDD

Row 12: Purl.

Row 13: K2, center single out, k3, center single in, k2.

   Center Single Out, Center Single In

Row 14: Purl—11 sts.

See also: **BAG OF TRICKS** DECREASE IN STYLE

Increase and Decrease Swatch Chart

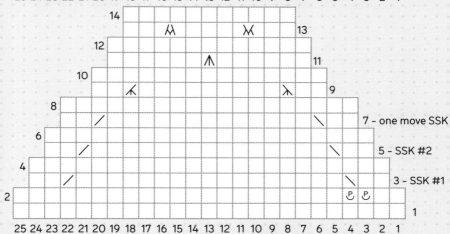

Key

☐	RS: knit / WS: purl
●	RS: purl / WS: knit
Ɛ	Eastern Purl
＼	SSK
／	K2tog
⋌	SK2P
⋏	K3tog
⋀	CDD
⋈	Central Single – Out
⋈	Central Single – In

Special Abbreviations

- **CDD (central double decrease):** Slip two stitches as if doing a K2TOG, knit 1, pass two slipped stitches over.

- **CS – Lean Out:** Center Single lean out.

- **CS – Lean In:** Center Single lean in.

- **K3TOG:** Knit three stitches together as one.

- **KFB:** Knit into front and back of stitch.

- **SK2P:** Slip one, knit two together, pass slipped stitch over the K2TOG.

- **SSK:** Slip two stitches individually as if to knit. Knit the two slipped stitches together.

SWATCHSERVATIONS

What do you think of each decrease? Which one looks best? Was that decrease easier for you to work than the traditional version?

Color the knitting needle to rank tricks 1—4!

One-Move SSK

SK2P

K3TOG

CDD

....
....
....
....

Center Single Lean Out

....
....
....
....

Center Single Lean In

....
....
....
....

You've had fun with decreases, so now it's time to play with our increases. Again, you'll find both written instructions and a chart so you can use whichever you prefer. You should have 11 stitches on your needles.

CONTINUE WITH SWATCH #6

(continued from decrease swatch; use in Lessons 6 and 7)

Row 15: Knit.

Row 16: Purl.

Row 17: K4, p1, yo, k1, yo, p1, k4—13 sts.

> *YOs take traditional path.*
> *These will not match in size.*

Row 18: P4, k1, p3, k1, p4.

Row 19: K2, k2tog, p2, YO, k1, B-YO, p2, SSK, k2.

> *YOs take short path.*
> *These will match in size.*

Row 20: (P3, k2) × 2, p3.

Row 21: K1, K2TOG, p3, B-YO, k1, yo, p3, SSK, k1.

> *YOs take longer path.*
> *These will match in size.*

Row 22: P2, k3, p3, k3, p2.

Row 23: Knit.

Row 24: Purl.

Row 25: K2, M1L, k9, M1R, k2—15 sts.

> *Traditional M1*

Row 26: Purl.

Row 27: K2, EL Left, k11, EL Right, k2—17 sts.

> *E-loop version of M1*

Row 28: Purl.

Row 29: K2, yo, k13, B-YO, k2—19 sts.

Row 30: P16, p tbl, p2.

> *Twisted YO version of M1*

Row 31: K1, Kfsl, k14, kfb, k2—21 sts.

Row 32: Purl.

Row 33: Knit.

Row 34: Purl.

Row 35: K2, LLI, k17, RLI, k2—23 sts.

Row 36: Purl.

Row 37: Knit.

Row 38: P1, Pfsl, p21—24 sts.

Row 39: K2, LLI, k22—25 sts.

Row 40: Purl.

Don't bind off (you'll use this swatch again in Lesson 7).

See also: **BAG OF TRICKS** THE PERFECT ADDITION

Increase and Decrease Swatch Chart

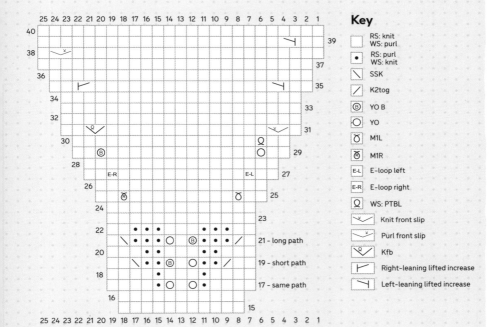

Special Abbreviations

- **KFB:** Knit into front and back of stitch.
- **KFSL:** Knit into front of stitch, slip back of stitch.
- **LLI (left lifted increase):** Insert tip of LH needle under the second purl bump below the stitch just knitted. Knit this through the back loop.
- **M1L (make 1 left):** Insert tip of LH needle from front to back under horizontal strand between last stitch worked and next stitch on LH needle, knit lifted strand through back loop.

- **M1R (make 1 right):** Insert tip of LH needle from back to front under horizontal strand between last stitch worked and next stitch on LH needle, knit lifted strand through front loop.
- **PFSL:** Knit into front of stitch, slip back of stitch.
- **PTBL:** Purl through the back loop.
- **RLI (right lifted increase):** Insert tip of RH needle into the purl bump below the first stitch on the left needle, lifting it onto the LH needle. Knit this new stitch through the front loop.
- **YOB:** Yarnover backwards.

SWATCHSERVATIONS

What do you think of each increase? Which one looks best?
Was it easier for you to work than the traditional version?

Do you have a
project in mind that
might use these?

Color the skein
sections to rank
the tricks 1—4!

YO—Short Path

YO—Long Path

M1 Left and Right (Twisted YO Version)

Left Lifted Increase (LLI)

Right Lifted Increase (RLI)

KFSL (Row Below LLI)

KFSL and PFSL (Row Below RLI)

PICTURES & THOUGHTS

what did you learn
about your knitting?

Do you have
a favorite
decrease trick?

Do you have
a favorite
increase trick?

Notes

....

....

....

....

....

....

....

....

....

....

....

...How it's going

KNITMOJI
STICKER
HERE

—

DID YOU MAKE A MISTAKE...

OR DID YOU INVENT A NEW STITCH

Embrace The Why and The Why Not

Now that you have thoroughly explored your knits and purls, improved your knitting technique, experimented with your gauge, explored new fibers, mastered your cast-ons, and played with increases and decreases, it's time to really dig into your specialized techniques.

Although a few of these swatches will look like mini sweaters, don't be fooled. You'll be exploring techniques that can be applied to any project.

As you work through these jam-packed exercises, remember you'll be practicing tricks that might not be listed in a pattern. That doesn't mean you can't bring your mad skills to the table and do things a bit differently. From different ways to join a new ball, through circular tricks, ribbing hacks, and perfect shaping, these tricks are yours to apply as you see fit.

There are a lot of tricks in this lesson, so take your time working through these exercises. It's not about the destination. It's about the journey. As you knit, start thinking about projects in which you'll use these newly perfected techniques.

Scoop up your swatches in progress and let's perfect our knitting.

EXERCISE: JOINING A NEW BALL AND FIXING THE FIRST STITCH

First up, grab your Swatch #1 in progress and a skein of non-superwash wool in a second color. It's time to practice cleaning up your first stitch and to discover the many ways to join a new ball.

CONTINUE SWATCH #1

Tighten the first stitch of the row (which is really the last stitch of the row below).

Next row (RS): Fix that first stitch; knit to end of row.

Row 2 (WS): Purl.

Join new ball in the middle of the row:

Row 3 (RS): K10, break yarn. Join the new ball (color B) in middle of row; knit to end of row.

Measure how much yarn you need for a row:

Row 4 (WS): Test how much yarn you need to get across a row; measure; tie knot. Purl.

Row 5 (RS): If you hit the knot, measure out a bit more yarn and try again. Knit.

Row 6 (WS): Purl to end of row. Break yarn, leaving tail.

Join a new ball in the middle of the row and knit in tail:

Row 7 (RS): Join new ball (color A), trap it and knit in the tail of color B.

Row 8 (WS): Purl.

Add a new color using the felted join:

Row 9 (RS): Knit to end of row, then tink back halfway and try out the felted join to change colors. Join color B back to color A.

Row 10 (WS): Purl and watch the color change.

Row 11 (RS): Knit.

Row 12 (WS): Purl.

BO and weave in the ends.

SWATCHSERVATIONS

What do you think of fixing the first stitch and the different methods to join a new ball?

Color the knitting needle to rank tricks 1–4!

Tightening the First Stitch

....

....

Joining Yarn in the Middle of the Row

....

....

Measuring out Yarn for a Row

....

....

Join at the Start of Row and Trap

....

....

Knitting in Your Tail as You Go

....

....

Felted Join

....

....

PICTURES & THOUGHTS

What are some projects that might use these joins?

Did you try knitting in the tail more than one way?

Notes

....

....

....

....

....

....

....

....

....

← Felted Join

← Start of Row Join

← Middle of Row Join

EXERCISE: CIRCULAR TRICKS (PART ONE) — JOGLESS CAST-ON AND SHORT-ROW JOIN

Ready to rock your circular tricks? Grab a needle (or needles) suitable to work a small circumference (DPN, magic loop, two circs – your choice) and a worsted weight or heavier yarn in light main color and a small amount of two contrasting colors.

We'll start with your jogless join. Short row knitters, choose W&T or German short row, or cast on twice and work them both. If you prefer to eliminate the short rows, work a few rounds of stockinette after your join and skip to the next exercise.

SWATCH #10

JOGLESS JOIN & JOGLESS PURL STRIPE

Using long tail cast-on, CO 37 sts.

Join for knitting in the round; place marker, using the join-in-round trick; knit last 2 sts tog – 36 sts.

Purl one round.

Use the jogless purl trick by slipping the first purl stitch from LH needle to RH needle, then return the end of round marker (it has moved over one stitch).

See also: **BAG OF TRICKS** CIRCULAR KNITTING: ROUND AND ROUND WE GO

Jogless Join and Jogless Purl Row

NOTE: See *Bag of Tricks* Resources for a review of the Wrap and Turn and German Short Row.

OPTION 1: WRAP AND TURN METHOD

Short-Row Set 1

Row 1 (RS): K18, pm for side, k12, W&T.

Row 2 (WS): P6, W&T.

NOTE: When working short row shaping, close each previous doubled stitch as you come to it by working it with its wrap before the next W&T.

Short-Row Set 2

Row 3 (RS): Work to 2 sts past last wrap, W&T.

Row 4 (WS): Work to 2 sts past last wrap, W&T.

Short-Row Set 3

Row 5 (RS): Work to 1 st past last wrap, W&T.

Row 6 (WS): Work to 1 st past last wrap, W&T.

Closing Round

Row 7 (RS): Knit to end of round, working last RS wrap as you come to it.

Row 8 (final closing rnd): Close final WS W&T, using the trick to close without a gap. Work to the end of the round.

W&T with no gap

OPTION 2: GERMAN SHORT ROWS

Short-Row Set 1

Row 1 (RS): K18, pm for side, k12, turn.

Row 2 (WS): Doubled Stitch (DS), p5, turn.

NOTE: When working short-row shaping, close each previous doubled stitch as you come to it by working it as a K2TOG or P2TOG before the next turn and DS.

Short-Row Set 2

Row 3 (RS): DS, work to 3 sts past DS, turn.

Row 4 (WS): DS, work to 3 sts past DS, turn.

Short-Row Set 3

Row 5 (RS): DS, work to 2 sts past DS, turn.

Row 6 (WS): DS, work to 2 sts past DS, turn.

Closing Round

Row 7 (RS): DS, then knit to end of rnd, working last right-side DS together.

Row 8 (final closing rnd): Close final (WS) DS using the trick to close without a hole. Work to end of rnd.

Work five more rounds in stockinette.

Don't bind off; you will continue working with this swatch below.

See also: **BAG OF TRICKS** SHORT ROW IN THE ROUND

German Short Row with no hole

...How it's going

KNITMOJI STICKER HERE

SWATCHSERVATIONS

What do you think of the tricks?

Jogless Join for Cast-On

Color the skein sections to rank the tricks 1—4!

Did you try both short-row techniques?   Yes ☐   No ☐

Short Row Circular Join (W&T)

Short Row Circular Join (German Short Row)

PICTURES & THOUGHTS

What do you think
of short rows?

Do you have a
favorite short
row method?

What projects would
use short rows?

DON'T FORGET
YOUR STICKERS!

Continue on your journey by adding another jogless garter stripe, this time in another color, and then move on to your two-round and single round stripes.

SWATCH #10 *[CONTINUED]*

JOGLESS GARTER

Next rnd: Join color B and purl one full rnd.

Next rnd (jogless garter): Remove end of rnd marker, sl first st purlwise from LH needle to RH needle, return end of rnd marker (it has moved over one stitch), knit one full rnd.

JOGLESS TWO-ROUND STOCKINETTE STRIPE

Next rnd: Return to color A. Knit one rnd.

Next rnd (jogless two-row): Remove end of rnd marker, work into the row below of first stitch, replace end of rnd marker, knit to end of rnd.

Knit three more rnds of color A.

Don't bind off; you will continue working this swatch.

SINGLE ROUND STRIPES

Next rnd: Slide sts from one needle to another to move away from end of rnd marker. Join color B. Work a single-rnd stripe. Join ring of color B.

Next rnd: Slide sts from one needle to another to move away from the color B join. Join color C. Work single rnd stripe, working final step to close color B. Join ring of color C.

Cut ends of colors B and C. Slide back to end of rnd marker to return to color A. Don't forget to work a two-row stripe when you return to color A.

See also: **BAG OF TRICKS** STRIPE SADNESS TO STRIPE GLADNESS

EXERCISE: CIRCULAR TRICKS (PART THREE) — SINGLE ROUND STRIPE AND JOGLESS BIND-OFF

Time to finish your circular swatch by adding another jogless stripe and practicing your jogless bind-off.

SWATCH #10 (CONTINUED)

JOGLESS TWO-ROUND STOCKINETTE STRIPE

Next rnd (jogless two-rnd): Remove end of rnd marker, work into the row below first st, replace end of rnd marker, knit to end of rnd.

Work three more rnds.

JOGLESS BIND-OFF

BO following the jogless trick.

Weave in your tail for cast-on and bind-off. Turn inside out, then weave in the tails of the color changes.

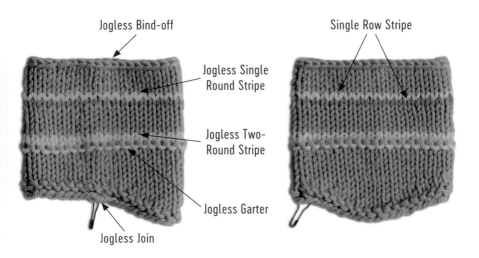

Jogless Bind-off

Jogless Single Round Stripe

Jogless Two-Round Stripe

Jogless Garter

Jogless Join

Single Row Stripe

SWATCHSERVATIONS

What do you think of the tricks?

Color the skein sections to rank the tricks 1–4!

Jogless Garter Stripe

....
....
....

Jogless Two-Round Stripe

....
....
....

Single-Round Stripe

....
....
....

Jogless Bind-Off

....
....
....

Do you have
a favorite
circular trick?

PICTURES & THOUGHTS

What did you think about
the circular tricks? Any
thoughts about using them
in upcoming projects?

Which ones need
some practice?

EXERCISE: PERFECT YOUR RIBBING

Time to bring out your swatch from Lesson 4 (you know, that long tail cast-on in pattern swatch). Before moving on to your mini sweater front, you'll get a chance to perfect your ribbing, by mending the gap, banning the blip, and fixing the flip!

You'll need swatch #7 (from Lesson 4), and a bit of contrasting yarn of the same weight.

SWATCH #7 *[CONTINUED FROM LESSON 4; USE IN LESSONS 6 & 7]*

MEND THE GAP — TIGHTEN UP RIB

Row 1 (RS): *K3, p2 (eastern); rep from * to last 3 sts, k3.

Row 2 (WS): *P3, k2tbl; rep from * to last 3 sts, p3.

BAN THE BLIP — FIX RIB STRIPE

Row 3 (RS): Join color B and knit.

Row 4 (WS): *P3, k2; rep from * to last 3 sts, p3.

Row 5 (RS): *K3, p2 (eastern); rep from * to last 3 sts, k3.

Row 6 (WS): P3, k2tbl; rep from * to last 3 sts, p3. Break color B.

Row 7 (RS): Return to MC, knit to end of row.

Row 8 (WS): *P3, k2; rep from * to last 3 sts, p3.

Row 9 (RS): *K3, p2 (eastern); rep from * to last 3 sts, k3.

 See also: **BAG OF TRICKS** NOT ALWAYS FOR OUR PLEASURE

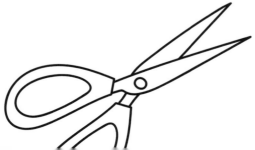

FIX THE FLIP — BETTER TRANSITION TO STOCKINETTE

Row 10 (WS): P1, sl2wyif, *k2tbl, sl3wyif; rep from * to last 5 sts, k2tbl, sl2wyif, p1.

Work in stockinette for 14 rows, ending with a WS row.

NOTE: Don't skip working the stockinette; we'll be using it to practice mattress stitch in Lesson 7.

Don't bind off; you will continue working with this swatch.

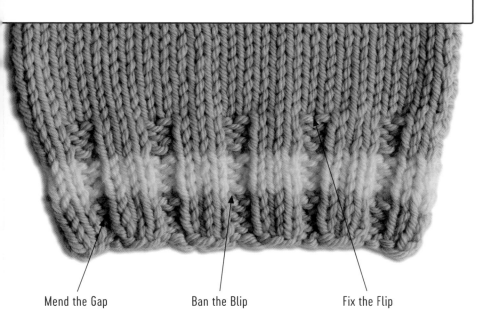

Mend the Gap   Ban the Blip   Fix the Flip

...How it's going

KNITMOJI STICKER HERE

SWATCHSERVATIONS
what do you think of the ribbing tricks?

Color the knitting needle to rank tricks 1—4!

Mend the Gap

....
....
....

Ban the Blip

....
....
....

Fix the Flip

....
....
....

Notes

....
....
....
....
....
....

How did your
ribbing change?

Can you think of
a project that
could use the
blipless stripe?

Do you work cables?
Would the rib trick help?

Finally, you'll complete your mini sweater front with a perfectly shaped neck.

Remember, these tricks are not just for a sweater: use them any time you bind off in the middle of the row, such as a keyhole opening for a scarf, a thumb for a fingerless mitt, etc.

When we have a pattern that requires you to bind off in the middle of the row, we get the gap, the dip, and the hole.

Here are the traditional instructions for a standard center bind-off:

Next row (RS): K11, join new ball, BO 6, knit to end of row — 11 sts for each shoulder.

SWATCH #7 *[CONTINUED FROM LESSON 4; USE IN LESSONS 6 & 7]*

NOTE: Both sides of the neck are worked simultaneously across a row, each with its own ball of yarn; a semicolon between pattern instructions separates the two sides.

Add a stitch (and then eliminate it) so there's no gap and dip!

PERFECT CENTER BO

Next row (RS): K11, **LL1, join new ball, k1, pass increased st over**, then BO 5 sts (don't forget to start with a knit one). To remove the sixth st, **slip first unworked st to RH needle, then work modified SSK.**

Your SSK gets rid of the chokehold at the end of the BO!

See also: **BAG OF TRICKS**   SWEATER SKILLS

SLOPED BIND-OFF

Row 2 (WS): Work to neck edge; BO 3 sts at neck edge, work to end of row.

Row 3 (RS): Work to neck edge; BO 3 sts at neck edge, work to end of row — 8 sts rem for each shoulder.

NOTE: To work the sloped BO: work the first two neck BOs as written, but use the sloped BO for the second pair.

Row 4 (WS): Work to neck edge; BO 2 sts at neck edge, work to end of row.

Row 5 (RS): Work to neck edge; BO 2 sts at neck edge, work to end of row — 6 sts rem for each shoulder.

Row 6 (WS): Purl both sides.

Row 7 (RS): Work to last 3 sts, K2TOG, k1; SSK, work to end of row — 5 sts rem for each shoulder.

Row 8 (WS): Purl both sides.

BO all rem shoulder sts.

Save this swatch for the next lesson. We'll block it and use it to practice seaming.

SWATCHSERVATIONS

What do you think of the perfect neck tricks?

Color the knitting needle to rank tricks 1–4!

Sloped Bind-Off

....

....

....

Perfect Center Bind-Off

....

....

....

PICTURES & THOUGHTS

When have you bound off in the center of a row?

Can you think of patterns that could use the sloped bind-off?

EXERCISE: SLOPED BIND-OFF AND CAST-ON

You tried a couple of sloped bind-offs on your neck. Now you can practice them again and create some sloped cast-ons. Here you're creating a mini dolman sweater sleeve, but there are many patterns that use stacked cast-ons. Give them a try.

You'll be finishing off the swatch you started in Lesson 4. You've already worked your perfect 1x1 rib and some stockinette, so it's time to jump right into your sleeves.

SWATCH #9 *(CONTINUED FROM LESSON 4)*

SLOPED CAST-ON

Next row (RS): Using cable cast-on, CO 3 sts and work to end of row.

Row 2 (WS): Using cable cast-on purl, CO 3 sts and work to end of row — 27 sts.

Rep last two rows two more times (using sloped cast-on trick) — 39 sts.

NOTE: On RS, use cable cast-on end trick knitwise. On WS, use cable cast-on end trick purlwise.

Work in stockinette for eight rows.

SLOPED BIND-OFF

BO 5 sts at beg of next six rows — 9 sts.

NOTE: To work the sloped bind-off, work the first sleeve bind-off as written, but use the sloped bind-off for the rest of sts.

BO rem neck sts.

See also: **BAG OF TRICKS** SLOPED CAST-ON

PICTURES & THOUGHTS

Was the sloped bind-off easier the second time?

When might you use the sloped cast-on?

...How it's going

KNITMOJI STICKER HERE

WHEN YOU FEEL
at loose ends
WEAVE
them in
AND KEEP
KNITTING!

Make a Great Last Impression

Do you have a bag of nearly finished projects sitting in the corner of a room taunting you? Or worse, have you been avoiding certain patterns because of some itty-bitty seam? Well, no more. It's time to get over the fear of finishing!

You've spent all this time perfecting your knitting, so don't stop now. In this final lesson, you'll get to practice your bind-off, blocking, weaving in ends, picking up stitches, mattress stitch, and even (if you dare) setting in a sleeve.

Once you finish this lesson, I hope you'll be inspired to open that bag of WIPs, throw your head back in defiant laughter, and declare "I'm not afraid of you!"

Don't just read about it; pick up your swatches and give it a try.

EXERCISE: BUILD A BETTER BIND-OFF

It's finally time to bind off Swatch #6, patiently waiting since Lesson 5. You'll square off the start by ditching the dip, then ban the choke hold and fix the end.

CONTINUE WITH SWATCH #6

BO 25 sts, making sure to:

☐ Ditch the dip: start with your YO trick
☐ Ban the choke hold: use your elastic bind-off
☐ Fix the end: work into the row below

SWATCHSERVATIONS

How do you like your square start and end?

Was your bind-off elastic enough to allow your swatch to curve?

EXERCISE: BLOCKING AND WEAVING IN ENDS

You have already knit one mini sweater front and in this lesson, you'll knit a second piece. Then you'll use these two pieces to practice your blocking and seaming.

For this lesson, you'll need Swatch #7, Swatch #8, a tapestry needle, and scissors.

CONTINUE WITH SWATCH #8

Work in stockinette for 10 more rows, ending with a WS row.

BEGIN NECK DECREASES

Next row (RS): K2, SSK, work to end – 14 sts.

Next row (WS): Purl.

Rep last 2 rows 7 more times – 7 sts.

BO all rem sts.

CONTINUE WITH SWATCHES #7 & #8

NOTE: Take pictures of swatches 7 and 8 before you block and after you block.

WEAVE IN ENDS

Try weaving some in before you block and some after. What is the difference?
Don't clip the tail until after your blocking is complete.

BLOCK

Block according to the ball band. If it's wool, try a nice wet block.

CLIP ENDS

After your piece is dry, clip and fan the ends of your yarn tails.

NOTE: These two swatches have the same number of rows. They will be seamed together later in the lesson.

See also: **BAG OF TRICKS** BLOCKING AND WEAVING IN ENDS

SWATCHSERVATIONS

How did weaving in ends go?

What did you think of weaving in ends before versus after blocking?

What did you think of clipping the ends? Do you think they will stay put?

SWATCH #7
(UNBLOCKED)

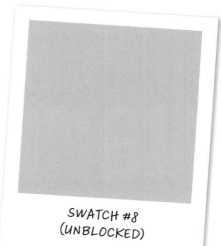

SWATCH #8
(UNBLOCKED)

PICTURES & THOUGHTS

Was it easy to block the two pieces to the same height?

What was the difference between the unblocked and blocked swatch?

SWATCH #7
(BLOCKED)

SWATCH #8
(BLOCKED)

EXERCISE: MATTRESS STITCH

If you've never done mattress stitch, get ready to feel like a magician. I'll never forget the feeling when I "zipped" that first seam shut. I literally said out loud "COOL!" — then asked the friend who taught me, "Why have I been avoiding seaming all this time?"

Don't forget your secret start to make sure the edges line up.

For this lesson, you'll need Swatch #7, Swatch #8, a tapestry needle, and scissors.

CONTINUE WITH SWATCHES #7 AND #8

Join the straight sides of Swatches #7 and #8 together.

☐ Use the figure-eight join.

☐ Use the secret start.

SWATCHSERVATIONS

What do you think of your figure-eight join and mattress stitch?

 Color the skein sections to rank the tricks 1—4!

Figure-Eight Join

....

....

....

Mattress Stitch with Secret Start

....

....

....

POOF!

...How it's going

EXERCISE: CALCULATE THE PERFECT PICK-UP

You are the boss of your knitting! You don't have to pick up the number of stitches called for in the pattern. Your stitch or row gauge might be different or you may have changed the garment length. You'll get a much better-looking result if you pick up the number of stitches right for your knitting.

You can take several paths to calculate your perfect pick-up. Try them out!

METHOD #1: USE YOUR GAUGE AND YOUR MEASUREMENTS

This is a great option if your stitch gauge is different from the pattern or if you've changed the sweater length.

You'll have to measure your trim stitch gauge.

- Your cardigan opening is 18in/46cm.
- Your trim stitch gauge is 5½ stitches per 1in/2.5cm

First calculate the number of stitches picked up based on gauge.

☐ *(stitch gauge)* × ☐ in/cm = ☐ sts

How many stitches would you pick up for a 2x2 rib (a multiple of 4 + 2)? ☐ sts

[ANSWERS ON PAGE 130]

(k2,p1)   every other row   42   17 rounds

METHOD #2: USE THE PATTERN

This is a great option if your gauge is the same, but you've changed the length. You can use your sweater as a guide.

- The cardigan opening in the pattern is 18in/46cm.
- Pick-up is 1x1 rib, starting and ending with a knit stitch (multiple of 2 + 1).
- Pattern pick-up is 107 sts.

How many stitches per in/cm in the pattern?

☐ sts ÷ ☐ in/cm = ☐ sts

Say you'd like a shorter cardigan, with an opening of 16in/40.5cm.

☐ sts ÷ ☐ in/cm = ☐ sts

How many stitches would you pick up for a 1x1 rib (multiple of 2 + 1)? ☐ sts

(ANSWERS ON PAGE 130)

See also: **BAG OF TRICKS**   PICKING UP STITCHES/GOING ROGUE

repeat from
decrease

?

sts/in

√?

EXERCISE: THE PICK-UP

Now that you're comfortable with calculating a perfect pick-up, let's put it into practice.

See also: **BAG OF TRICKS** PICKING UP STITCHES/GOING ROGUE

For this lesson, you'll need Swatch #8, locking stitch markers, and a needle one or two sizes smaller than you used to knit Swatch #8.

CONTINUE SWATCH #8

Now continue working with Swatch #8, remembering the pick-up tricks you want to practice:

☐ Stab it out to plan it out

☐ Fix the swoosh

☐ Round the corner

STEP 1: STAB IT OUT TO PLAN IT OUT

For your swatch, you'll want to pick up a multiple of 4 + 3 stitches (approximately 27 or 31 sts). Count every available pick-up space. Don't forget to factor into your final stitch count the two YOs at the corner (e.g., if you thought 31 stitches was perfect for you, you'd be picking up 29 stitches plus two YOs). Decide how many spaces you'll skip and how to spread them out.

STEP 2: FIX THE SWOOSH AND ROLL

Pick up your lowest stitch right above the cast-on edge.

Round the corner

Place a locking stitch marker at the point of the v-neck, pick up to the marker, make a YO, remove marker, pick up a stitch in the corner, make a YO, complete your pick-up, making sure you have a multiple of 4 + 3.

Now let's blitz that band:

Row 1 (WS): *P2, k2, rep from * to last 3 sts, p3 (remembering to work those YOs through the back loop).

SWATCHSERVATIONS

How did your pick-up go?

Color the skein
sections to rank
the tricks 1—4!

Stab it out to plan it out

....

....

....

Fix the swoosh

....

....

....

Round the corner

....

....

....

EXERCISE: THE PERFECT BUTTONHOLE

What button band would be complete without the perfect buttonhole? We know that using the traditional approach can give a less-than-stellar result. Do you remember why?

Hint: You already saw some of these problems in the neck bind-off.

Here are the traditional instructions for a two-stitch buttonhole:

First buttonhole row (RS): K2, p2, k2, BO 2 sts, cont in patt to end of row.

Next buttonhole row (WS): Knit the knits and purl the purls until you reach the buttonhole gap, CO 2 sts, cont in patt to end of row.

What do you get?

| Gap and Dip (beg of BO) | + | chokehold (end of BO) | + | Gap (CO) | = *HOT MESS* |

Grab Swatch #8 and don't hit the panic button — we're going to fix the faults and create buttonhole perfection.

See also: **BAG OF TRICKS** BEST BUTTONHOLE EVER

Buttonhole

Add a stitch (and then eliminate it) so there's no gap and dip!

TWO-STITCH BUTTONHOLE TRICK

First buttonhole row (RS): K3, p2, k1, **kfb**, purl next st and pass the increased stitch over, BO 1 st, pass last st worked to LH needle, **K2TOG**; continue working in pattern to end of row.

Your K2TOG gets rid of the chokehold at the end of the BO!

Next row (WS): Knit the knits and purl the purls until you reach the buttonhole gap, using e-loop cast-on, CO 1 st, work in patt as established to end of row.

Next row (RS): Work in patt to buttonhole, **use the strand to create a second e-loop**, work in patt to end of row.

Next row (WS): Work in pattern.

BO in pattern.

Block button band.

No gap here either!

...How it's going

KNITMOJI STICKER HERE

SWATCHSERVATIONS

How did your button band go?

Rank the tricks by adding expressions to the buttons!

Pick-up with extra stitch at bottom of band

....

....

....

Round the curve with extra YO

....

....

....

Perfect buttonhole

....

....

....

PICTURES & THOUGHTS

what do you think of your button band after blocking?

Can you see your buttonhole when it's closed?

Notes

....

....

....

....

....

Even if you think you'll never knit a sweater, give this a try. Often it's fear of seaming, and specifically, setting in a sleeve, that keeps knitters from the sweater of their dreams.

Before you can grab your tailor's ham, you'll knit two tiny armholes and a sleeve cap. Make sure you use the same yarn for all three. You'll see my gauge; if you are knitting to a different gauge, the important thing to know is the cap height should be about two-thirds the height of the armhole.

You'll also need a tapestry needle, locking stitch markers, seaming yarn, and scissors.

SWATCH #11: SLEEVE CAP

Patty's Gauge: 20 sts & 28 rows per 4in/10cm

CO 42 sts using the long tail cast-on.

Starting with a WS row, work three rows in stockinette.

BO 4 sts at beg of next 2 rows — 34 sts.

Next row (RS/dec row): K2, K2TOG, work to last 4 sts, SSK, k2 — 32 sts.

Rep decr row every RS row two more times, followed by every 4th row three more times and every RS row three more times — 16 sts.

BO 2 sts at beg of next 4 rows — 8 sts.

BO rem 8 sts.

Scan the QR code to watch a video of Patty setting in a sleeve:

ARMHOLE #1

Patty's Gauge: 20 sts & 28 rows per 4in/10cm

CO 20 sts.

Starting with a WS row, work three rows in stockinette.

Next row (RS): BO 4 sts, work to end of row — 16 sts.

Row 2 (WS): Purl.

Row 3 (RS): K2, K2TOG, work to end of row — 15 sts.

Rep dec row every RS row three more times — 12 sts.

Work straight in stockinette stitch until armhole measures approx. 6in/15cm, ending with a WS row.

SHAPE SHOULDERS

BO 4 sts at beg of next three RS rows.

ARMHOLE #2

Patty's Gauge: 20 sts & 28 rows per 4in/10cm

CO 20 sts.

Starting with a WS row, work four rows in stockinette.

Next row (WS): BO 4 sts, work to end — 16 sts.

Knit to last 4 sts, SSK, k2 — 15 sts.

Rep dec row every RS row three more times — 12 sts.

Work straight in stockinette until armhole measures approx. 6in/15cm, ending with a RS row.

SHAPE SHOULDERS

BO 4 sts at beg of next three WS rows.

Block all three pieces.

Seam shoulders together. Set in the sleeve.

See also: **BAG OF TRICKS** SETTING IN A SLEEVE

PICTURES & THOUGHTS

How were the
measurements
of your pieces?

Have you ever knit a
set-in sleeve sweater?

FINISHED SLEEVE CAP

DON'T FORGET
YOUR STICKERS!

what did you think of seaming?

SLEEVE CAP SELFIE

Did the ham help?

—

When you don't know what you 'can't' knit…

YOU CAN KNIT

ANY THI NG!

The Great Journey Begins

Now that you've finished the exercises, the REAL fun begins.

At the end of *Patty Lyons' Knitting Bag of Tricks*,
I left you with five bits of advice:

Learn to read
your knitting.

Understand
how it's built.

Don't make the same
mistake twice;
make different
mistakes.

Fight for
the why.

And the most important one,
what this workbook is all about:

TAKE
OWNERSHIP
OF YOUR
KNITTING.

I hope working through these exercises has helped you in that journey.
This workbook is here for you to grow with as you track your progress.

In the "My Work" section, you'll have room to record your projects,
your knitting goals, and what tricks you are going to use.

I can't wait to see what you knit next.

ANSWERS...

PAGE 36: THE THREE MAGIC FACTORS

1. Formula: $\boxed{200}$ (what: $\boxed{\text{sts}}$) ÷ $\boxed{40}$ (what: $\boxed{\text{in}}$) = $\boxed{5}$ (gauge)

2. Formula: $\boxed{8}$ (what: $\boxed{\text{in}}$) × $\boxed{5}$ (what: $\boxed{\textit{gauge}}$) = $\boxed{40}$ (stitches)

3. Formula: $\boxed{200}$ (what: $\boxed{\text{sts}}$) ÷ $\boxed{5.25}$ (what: $\boxed{\textit{gauge}}$) = $\boxed{38/96.5}$ (in/cm)

PAGE 37: SIZE ADJUSTMENTS WITH GAUGE

1. Overall size change

Since your gauge is LARGER than the patterns, to get an in-between size, which size should you try at your gauge — the second (99 stitches) or the third (110 stitches)?

$\boxed{99}$ sts

What will the width of the sweater back be in inches/centimeters when worked in your gauge?

Formula: $\boxed{99}$ (what: $\boxed{\text{sts}}$) ÷ $\boxed{5.25}$ (what: $\boxed{\textit{gauge}}$) = $\boxed{18.9/48}$ (in/cm)

2. Change a portion of the sweater

Formula: $\boxed{99}$ (what: $\boxed{\text{sts}}$) ÷ $\boxed{19}$ (what: $\boxed{\text{in}}$) = $\boxed{5.21}$ (gauge)

(Rounded) How many stitches per 4in/10cm? $\boxed{21}$ sts]

PAGE 38: MISSING GAUGE INFORMATION

1. Overall gauge

Formula: $\boxed{129}$ (what: $\boxed{\text{sts}}$) ×⊘ $\boxed{19}$ (what: $\boxed{\text{in}}$) = $\boxed{6.8}$ (gauge)

(Rounded) How many stitches per 4in/10cm = $\boxed{27}$

PAGE 39: ROW GAUGE

1. Same shape, different row gauge

How many rows were used in the shaping zone after the first decrease?

5 times × [8] (rows) = [40] rows total

How many inches/centimeters are in the shaping zone using the pattern gauge?

[40] (rows) ÷ [7] (gauge) = [5.7/14.5] in/cm

How many rows in YOUR gauge are in the shaping zone?

[5.7] (inches) × [6] (gauge) = [34] rows

Divide number of rows in your shaping zone by the number of shaping rows in your gauge.

Spread out the five remaining decreases to waist:

[34] (rows) ÷ [5] (shaping rows) = [6.8] rows to repeat

Round down to nearest even number.

Repeat decrease row every [6] rows 5 more times.

PAGE 40: ROW GAUGE

2. Different length, different row gauge

How many rows were used in the shaping zone after the first decrease?

9 times × [12] (rows) = [108] rows total

How many inches/centimeters are in the shaping zone?

[108] (rows) ÷ [7] (gauge) = [15.4/39] (in/cm)

How many inches/centimeters are in YOUR shaping zone?

[15.4/39] (pattern shaping zone) − [2/5] (in/cm you're removing) = [13.4/34] (in/cm)

How many rows in YOUR gauge are in YOUR shaping zone?

[13.4/34] (in/cm) × [6] (gauge) = [80.4] (rounded down to even number) [80] rows

Divide number of rows in shaping zone by number of shaping rows

Spread out nine remaining increases for sleeve:

$\boxed{80}$ (rows) ÷ 9 (shaping rows) = $\boxed{8.8}$ rows to repeat

Round down to the nearest even number.

Repeat decrease row every $\boxed{8}$ rows nine more times

How many inches/centimeters are used in your final shaping zone?

9 (remaining shaping rows) × $\boxed{8}$ (repeat) = $\boxed{72}$ total rows used

72 total rows used ÷ $\boxed{6}$ (your row gauge) = $\boxed{12/30.5}$ (in/cm)

PAGE 112: CALCULATE THE PERFECT PICK-UP

1. Use your gauge and your measurements

First calculate the number of stitches picked up based on gauge.

$\boxed{5.5}$ (stitch gauge) × $\boxed{18/46}$ in/cm = $\boxed{99}$ sts

How many stitches would you pick up for a 2x2 rib (a multiple of 4 + 2)? $\boxed{98}$ sts

2. Use the pattern

How many stitches per in/cm in the pattern?

$\boxed{107}$ sts ÷ $\boxed{18/46}$ in/cm = $\boxed{5.94}$ sts

Say you'd like a shorter cardigan, with an opening of 16in/40.5cm.

$\boxed{5.94}$ sts × $\boxed{16/40.5}$ in/cm = $\boxed{95.04}$ sts

How many stitches would you pick up for a 1x1 rib (multiple of 2 + 1)? $\boxed{95}$ sts

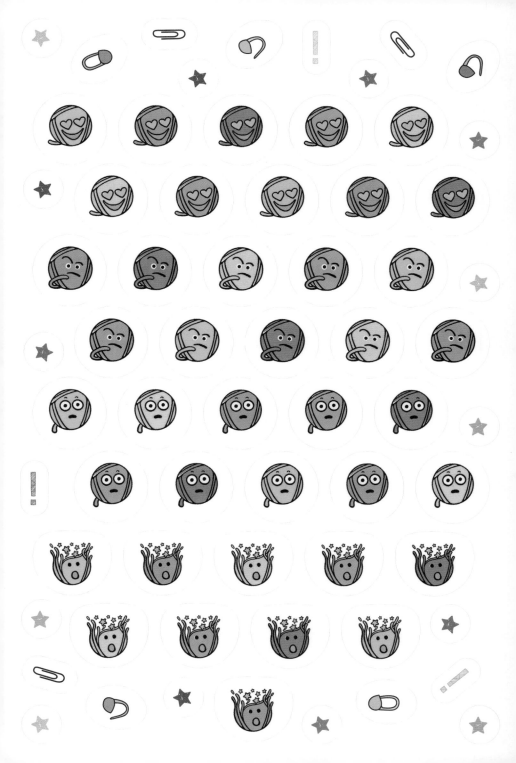

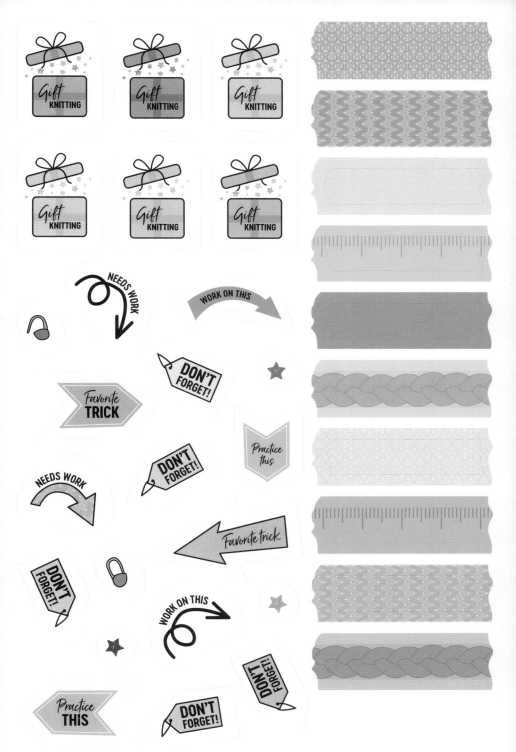

Dress Up
YOUR SHEEP

NEEDLE INVENTORY

METRIC (MM)	US	UK	SINGLE POINT	DPN	CIRCULAR					
					8in/ 20cm	16in/ 40cm	24in/ 60cm	36in/ 91cm	40in/ 101cm	60in/ 152cm
0.5	8-0	24								
0.75	6-0	22								
		20								
1.0	5-0	19								
1.25	4-0	18								
1.5	000	17								
		16								
1.75	00	15								
2	0	14								
2.25	1	13								
2.5	1.5									
2.75	2	12								
3	2.5	11								
3.25	3	10								
3.5	4									
3.75	5	9								
4	6	8								
4.25										
4.5	7	7								
4.75										
5	8	6								
5.25										
5.5	9	5								
5.75										
6	10	4								
6.5	10.5	3								
7		2								
7.5		1								
8	11	0								
9	13	00								
10	15	000								
12	17	4-0								
15	19	5-0								
19	35									
25	50									

—

AnKNITcipation

{an-nit-sip-a-shun}

noun.

1. A knitter waiting to cast on.

Twelve Months — Twelve Projects

We all enjoy many types of knitting. There's our "I want to wear that" knitting, our gift knitting, and our mindless zen knitting. The following twelve project pages are for you to track your year of skill-building knitting. Pick out twelve projects, then think about the techniques featured and the tricks from the book you'll use.

Siince you may want to knit more than twelve, here's a place to list all the other projects you want to tackle and what skills you'll use:

PROJECT NAME	SKILLS USED

Project Name

Cast on: Finished:

TECHNIQUES USED

Tips to use

MEASUREMENTS

Gauge: [   ] sts per 4in/10cm

[   ] rows per 4in/10cm

Other gauge (motif width):

Size knit:

New skills learned

MATERIALS

Add sample yarn snips

Yarn:

Number of skeins used:

Needles:

Notions:

PROJECT NOTES

Tah dah! The finished project photo!

Project Name

....

Cast on: .... Finished: ....

TECHNIQUES USED

Tips to use

MEASUREMENTS

Gauge: [　　] sts per 4in/10cm

[　　] rows per 4in/10cm

Other gauge (motif width):

Size knit:
....

New skills learned

MATERIALS

Add sample yarn snips

Yarn:
....

Number of skeins used:
....

Needles:
....

Notions:
....

PROJECT NOTES

....

....

....

....

....

....

....

....

....

....

....

....

....

Tah dah! The finished project photo!

Project Name

....

KNITMOJI
STICKER
HERE

Cast on:
....

Finished:
....

TECHNIQUES USED

Tips to use

MEASUREMENTS

Gauge: [ ] sts per 4in/10cm

[ ] rows per 4in/10cm

Other gauge (motif width):
....

Size knit:
....

New skills learned

MATERIALS

Add sample yarn snips

Yarn:
....

Number of skeins used:
....

Needles:
....

Notions:
....

138

PROJECT NOTES

....

....

....

....

....

....

....

....

....

....

....

....

....

....

Tah dah! The finished
project photo!

Project Name

....

Cast on: ....   Finished: ....

KNITMOJI STICKER HERE

TECHNIQUES USED

Tips to use

MEASUREMENTS

Gauge: [ ] sts per 4in/10cm

[ ] rows per 4in/10cm

Other gauge (motif width): ....

Size Knit: ....

New skills learned

MATERIALS

Add sample yarn snips

Yarn: ....

Number of skeins used: ....

Needles: ....

Notions: ....

140

PROJECT NOTES

Tah dah! The finished
project photo!

Project Name

Cast on: Finished:

KNITMOJI
STICKER
HERE

TECHNIQUES USED

Tips to use

MEASUREMENTS

Gauge: [ ] sts per 4in/10cm

[ ] rows per 4in/10cm

Other gauge (motif width):

Size knit:

New skills learned

MATERIALS

Add sample yarn snips

Yarn:

Number of skeins used:

Needles:

Notions:

PROJECT NOTES

Tah dah! The finished project photo!

Project Name

....

KNITMOJI
STICKER
HERE

Cast on: .... Finished: ....

TECHNIQUES USED

Tips to use

MEASUREMENTS

Gauge: [ ] sts per 4in/10cm

[ ] rows per 4in/10cm

Other gauge (motif width): ....

Size knit: ....

New skills learned

MATERIALS

Add sample yarn snips

Yarn: ....

Number of skeins used: ....

Needles: ....

Notions: ....

Color me in to chart your progress!

Fix your swatch here or add a photo

PROJECT NOTES

Tah dah! The finished project photo!

Project Name

....

KNITMOJI
STICKER
HERE

Cast on: ....   Finished: ....

TECHNIQUES USED

Tips to use

MEASUREMENTS

Gauge: [ ] sts per 4in/10cm

[ ] rows per 4in/10cm

Other gauge (motif width):
....

Size Knit:
....

New skills learned

MATERIALS

Add sample yarn snips

Yarn:
....

Number of skeins used:
....

Needles:
....

Notions:
....

146

PROJECT NOTES

....

....

....

....

....

....

....

....

....

....

....

....

....

Tah dah! The finished project photo!

Project Name

KNITMOJI
STICKER
HERE

Cast on:

Finished:

TECHNIQUES USED

Tips to use

MEASUREMENTS

Gauge: ☐ sts per 4in/10cm

☐ rows per 4in/10cm

Other gauge (motif width):

Size knit:

New skills learned

MATERIALS

Add sample yarn snips

Yarn:

Number of skeins used:

Needles:

Notions:

Color me in to chart your progress!

Fix your swatch here or add a photo

PROJECT NOTES

Tah dah! The finished project photo!

Project Name

....

...How it went

KNITMOJI STICKER HERE

Cast on: ....

Finished: ....

TECHNIQUES USED

Tips to use

MEASUREMENTS

Gauge: [ ] sts per 4in/10cm

[ ] rows per 4in/10cm

Other gauge (motif width):
....

Size knit:
....

New skills learned

MATERIALS

Add sample yarn snips

Yarn:
....

Number of skeins used:
....

Needles:
....

Notions:
....

Color me in to chart your progress!

Fix your swatch here or add a photo

PROJECT NOTES

Tah dah! The finished project photo!

Project Name

....

Cast on: .... Finished: ....

KNITMOJI
STICKER
HERE

TECHNIQUES USED

Tips to use

MEASUREMENTS

Gauge: [   ] sts per 4in/10cm

[   ] rows per 4in/10cm

Other gauge (motif width): ....

Size knit: ....

New skills learned

MATERIALS

Add sample yarn snips

Yarn: ....

Number of skeins used: ....

Needles: ....

Notions: ....

PROJECT NOTES

....
....
....
....
....
....
....
....
....
....
....
....
....
....

Tah dah! The finished project photo!

Project Name

KNITMOJI STICKER HERE

Cast on:

Finished:

TECHNIQUES USED

Tips to use

MEASUREMENTS

Gauge: [ ] sts per 4in/10cm

[ ] rows per 4in/10cm

Other gauge (motif width):

Size Knit:

New skills learned

MATERIALS

Add sample yarn snips

Yarn:

Number of skeins used:

Needles:

Notions:

PROJECT NOTES

....
....
....
....
....
....
....
....
....
....
....
....
....
....

Tah dah! The finished project photo!

Project Name

.... *...How it went*

KNITMOJI
STICKER
HERE

Cast on: .... Finished: ....

TECHNIQUES USED

Tips to use

MEASUREMENTS

Gauge: [   ] sts per 4in/10cm

[   ] rows per 4in/10cm

Other gauge (motif width): ....

Size knit: ....

New skills learned

MATERIALS

Add sample yarn snips

Yarn: ....

Number of skeins used: ....

Needles: ....

Notions: ....

156

PROJECT NOTES

....

....

....

....

....

....

....

....

....

....

....

....

....

....

Tah dah! The finished project photo!

If You Can Dream It, You Can Knit It!

Now that you've knit your way through the workbook and finished the 12 skill-building projects, what's next? Use this space to list all your dream skills. What mountain will you climb next? Brioche, Estonian lace, double knitting? The sky's the limit.

Make your skill wish list here:

About The Author

PATTY LYONS is a nationally recognized knitting teacher and technique expert who is known for teaching the "why" not just the "how" in her pursuit of training the mindful knitter. She specializes in sweater design and sharing her love of the much-maligned subjects of gauge and blocking.

Patty's designs and knitting skill articles have been published in Vogue Knitting, Interweave Knits, Knit Purl, Knitter's Magazine, Cast On, Knit Style, Creative Knitting, Twist Collective, and Modern Daily Knitting where she writes a monthly knitter's advice column: "Ask Patty." Patty's designs have also been included in pattern collections from Classic Elite, Noro, Cascade, Tahki Stacy Charles, Sugar Bush, and Willow Yarns.

Patty is the author of the best-selling book: *Patty Lyons' Knitting Bag of Tricks.*

- **Learn about new classes and patterns:** pattylyons.com
- **Join the fun:** facebook.com/pattylyonsknitting/
- **Meet knitters:** ravelry.com/groups/the-patty-lyons-fan-club
- **Share your photos:** instagram.com/pattyjlyons (#pattylyonsbagoftricks)

Thank You to...

The entire team at David and Charles: Sarah Callard, Jeni Chown, and Anna Wade who brought the book to life. Thanks to the best knitting trio a girl could ask for: Carol Sulcoski, Linda Schmidt, and Franklin Habit. And a huge thank you to Zontee Hou and the whole team from Media Volery.

Dedicated to

Every knitter who has ever shared their time and talents with me in class. To every knitting student who pushed me by asking "why": I continue to learn from you every day.

Thank you!

A catalogue record for this book is available from the British Library.

ISBN-13: 9781446313558 hardback

This book has been printed on paper from approved suppliers and made from pulp from sustainable sources.

MIX
Paper | Supporting responsible forestry
FSC® C136333

Printed in China through Asia Pacific Offset, Ltd for David and Charles, Ltd, Suite A, Tourism House, Pynes Hill, Exeter, EX2 5WS

10 9 8 7 6 5 4 3 2 1

Publishing Director: Ame Verso
Senior Commissioning Editor: Sarah Callard
Managing Editor: Jeni Chown
Project Editor: Carol J. Sulcoski
Head of Design: Anna Wade
Pre-press Designer: Susan Reansbury
Illustrations: Franklin Habit
Technical Illustrations: Linda Schmidt
Photography: Jason Jenkins
Production Manager: Beverley Richardson

David and Charles publishes high-quality books on a wide range of subjects. For more information visit www.davidandcharles.com.

Share your makes with us on social media using #dandcbooks and follow us on Facebook and Instagram by searching for @dandcbooks.

Layout of the digital edition of this book may vary depending on reader hardware and display settings.